CURLS

Written and Illustrated

By:

Chelsea Heard

All SNUG and COZY in her bed,

Mackenzie Madison laid her head,

She walked and walked down the hall,

Her CURLS bouncing behind without
direction at all,

Mackenzie brushed and brushed and
brushed her teeth,

And hopped into the shower to get
SQUEAKY clean,

Mackenzie walked to her room back down the hall,

With a PULL and a TUG to get her shirt
over her CURLY CURLY Hair,

Mackenzie was finally dressed for school!

But now...what will she do with her
HAIR?

She BLOW DRIED her HAIR to get
it STRAIGHT,

But it stuck out HERE and THERE, in
EVERY WAY!

She wanted her CURLS to act HER WAY,
but Mackenzie's CURLS just wouldn't
BEHAVE!

So she stopped and thought, still holding her hair, "Why change my Curls, and their TWIST and TWIRL?"

So I'll go to school and ROCK my HAIR, and

wear my CURLS without a CARE!

And that's just what she did...so letting her
CURLS fly high and free, Mackenzie Madison
left for school, happy as could be!

The End

Now...

Draw You!

Draw you SLEEPING!

Draw you in the MORNING!

Draw you with your FRIENDS!

Draw you going to BED!

Draw your HAIR!

About the Author

Chelsea Heard is a 19 year-old graduate from Mt. Carmel High School in San Diego California, whose love, passion to help others and art helped her create this book. Much like Mackenzie Madison, Chelsea took her personal experiences with her curly hair, and created a relatable, fun, children's book, that would encourage young girls from all backgrounds to celebrate themselves, and be proud of who they are.